PHILIPPIANS
Chasing Happy

BIBLE STUDY GUIDE + STREAMING VIDEO

SIX SESSIONS

LORI WILHITE

HarperChristian Resources

Philippians Study Guide
© 2023 by Lori Wilhite

Requests for information should be addressed to:
HarperChristian Resources, 3900 Sparks Dr. SE, Grand Rapids, Michigan 49546

ISBN 978-0-310-13276-9 (softcover)
ISBN 978-0-310-13277-6 (ebook)

HarperChristian Resources titles may be purchased in bulk for church, business, fundraising, or ministry use. For information, please e-mail ResourceSpecialist@ChurchSource.com.

Author is represented by the literary agency of The FEDD Agency, Inc., Post Office Box 341973, Austin, Texas 78734.

First Printing May 2023 / Printed in the United States of America

CONTENTS

WELCOME

PHILIPPIANS

Chasing Happy

HAVE YOU EVER opened the Bible and felt overwhelmed? Have you ever wondered where to go for comfort and encouragement when you're feeling uncertain, confused, or disappointed in life? Which book of the Bible do you turn to for wisdom about the situation you find yourself in?

The *Beautiful Word Bible Studies* series makes the Bible come alive in such a way that you know where to turn no matter where you find yourself on your spiritual journey.

All of us are chasing happy in some form every day. We chase happy in our relationships, in the hunt for success, and through the next adventure. For all of our chasing, we only discover a dryness, a barrenness, a void that hardens our souls rather than filling them. Why? Because we're chasing the wrong kind of happy. We chase physical, emotional, and temporary happiness instead of the spiritual, eternal happiness found in Jesus.

Sometimes, we have a hard time believing God even wants us to be happy. I've heard it said that God cares more about our holiness than our happiness like the two are somehow disconnected. But what if the pursuit of happiness was actually adjacent to the pursuit of holiness?

The problem isn't that God doesn't want us to be happy. The problem is that we're chasing happy in the wrong things. Looking for it in all the wrong places. Happiness is ours when we chase God's joy, His purpose, His unity, His contentment, and His peace. Happy is captured when we chase Him.

That's a core message of the book of Philippians. This letter was written by Paul, when he was a prisoner in Rome, around 60 A.D., to the church he planted in the city of Philippi about ten years earlier.

Depending on the translation of the Bible you're using, the word "joy" or "rejoice" occurs at least fifteen times in just 104 verses. That's a lot of joy for a guy enduring house arrest, always chained to a Roman guard. And it's not just "joy" referenced; the name of Jesus is mentioned over forty times in the letter. So, yes, Philippians is the joy book of the Bible. But it is a joy, a happiness, that can clearly only be found in Jesus.

If you have ever struggled with laying hold of true happiness and joy, then this beautiful book is for you! You're invited to discover the incredible truth that happy isn't a work based on what we can do, but what God, through Christ, has already done. Happy isn't found in the circumstances around us, but in the power of Jesus in us. I can't wait to take off on this adventure through Philippians with you!

> • • • • •
>
> If you have ever **struggled** with laying hold of **true happiness** and **joy**, then this **beautiful** book is for **you!**
>
> • • • • •

HOW TO USE THIS GUIDE

GROUP INFORMATION AND SIZE RECOMMENDATIONS

The *Beautiful Word Philippians Bible Study* is designed to be experienced in a group setting such as a Bible study, small group, or other Sunday school class. Of course, you can always work through the material and watch the videos on your own if a group is unavailable. Maybe call a few friends or neighbors and start your own!

After opening with a short activity, you will watch each video session and participate in a time of group discussion and reflection on what you're learning both from the video teaching and the personal Bible study between meetings. This content is rich and takes you through the entire book, so be prepared for a full experience of the depth of Scripture.

If you have a larger group (more than twelve people), consider breaking up into smaller groups during the discussion time. It is important that members of the group can ask questions, share ideas and experiences, as well as feel heard and seen—no matter their backgrounds or circumstances.

MATERIALS NEEDED

Each participant should have his or her own study guide. Each study guide comes with individual streaming video access (instructions found on the inside front cover). Every member of your group has full access to watch videos from the convenience of their chosen devices at any time—for missed group meetings, for rewatching, for sharing teaching with others, or watching videos individually and then meeting if your group is short on meeting time—and that makes the group experience doable and more realistic. We have worked very hard to make gathering around the Word of God and studying accessible and simple.

This study guide includes video outline notes, group discussion questions, a personal Bible study section for between group meetings, Beautiful Word coloring pages, and Scripture memory cards to deepen learning between sessions.

There is a leader's guide in the back of each study guide so anyone can lead a group through this study. A lot of thought has been put into making the *Beautiful Word Bible Studies* series available to all—which includes making it easy to lead, no matter your experience or acumen!

TIMING

The timing notations—for example, twenty minutes—indicate the length of the video segments and the suggested times for each activity or discussion. Within your allotted group meeting time, you may not get to all the discussion questions. Remember that the *quantity* of questions addressed isn't as important as the *quality* of the discussion.

Using the leader's guide in the back of the guide to review the content overview of each session and the group discussion questions in advance will give you a good idea of which questions you want to focus on as a leader or group facilitator.

LEADING A GROUP

Each group should appoint a group leader who is responsible for starting the video and keeping track of time during the activities and discussion. Group leaders may also read questions aloud, monitor discussions, prompt participants to respond, and ensure that everyone has the opportunity to participate.

OPENING GROUP ACTIVITY

Depending on the amount of time you meet and the resources available, you'll want to begin the session with the group activity. You will find these activities on the group page that begins each session. The interactive icebreaker is designed to be a catalyst for group engagement and help participants prepare and transition to the ideas explored in the video teaching.

The leader or facilitator will want to read ahead to the following week's activity to see what will be needed and how participants may be able to contribute by bringing supplies or refreshments.

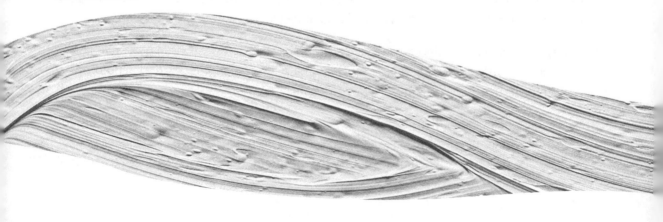

SESSION 1

CHASING
JOY

PHILIPPIANS

Opening Group Activity (10-15 MINUTES)

WHAT YOU WILL NEED:

* One sheet of blank paper for each person
* Pens, markers, and/or watercolors

   1. Use the paper and drawing/writing tools to create or write the word "Happy" in the center of the page. Next, jot down any specific things in life that make you feel happy.

   2. Share your words or phrases with each other as you discuss the following questions:

      What tends to make you feel happy in life?

      Which of these are healthy and good and life giving?

Watch Session One Video (25 MINUTES)

Group leader, stream the video (instructions are on the inside of the front cover of this guide) or play the DVD.

As you watch, take notes while thinking through:

What caught your attention? · · · · · · · · · · · · · · · ➤

What surprised you? · · · · · · · · · · · · · · · ➤

What made you reflect? · · · · · · · · · · · · · ➤

Happy is a work done from the inside out.

....

The beautiful and brutal moments of Paul

....

"Agape"— God's sacrificial, unconditional love

....

Mutual abiding produces fruit.

....

Battles with depression

....

Do one thing that brings joy.

....

SCRIPTURE COVERED IN THIS SESSION:
PHILIPPIANS 1:1–11

Group Discussion Questions (30–45 MINUTES)

Group leader, read each numbered prompt and question to the group and select volunteers for Scripture reading.

• • • • •

"**Happiness** will be ours, **joyfulness** will be found, **delight** will be experienced, **gladness** will be within our reach when we chase God's **joy**, His **purpose**, His **encouragement**, and His **peace**. Happy is captured when we chase Him." — Lori

• • • • •

What are some of the ways you've chased happy in unhealthy ways?

What are some of the ways you've chased happy in healthy, good ways?

1. **Select a volunteer to read the passage Philippians 1:3–6. Discuss the following:**

Where do you struggle to believe that the God who began a good work in you will bring it to completion?

How does the promise of Philippians 1:6 equip and empower you to chase happiness in the face of hardship?

"There were some really **beautiful** moments and some really **brutal** moments for Paul in Philippi. Paul could have thought back on his time with the Philippians and focused on his **painful** recovery from almost being **beaten** to death. He could have remembered the pain he felt and the **injustice** he faced. Yet, he says, '**every time** I think of you, I **thank God** and pray with joy.' Paul's **joy** wasn't anchored in the circumstances he encountered—good or bad. No, his joy was anchored in the '**grace** and **peace** that comes from God our Father and the Lord Jesus Christ'" (Philippians 1:2). — Lori

2. **On a scale of one to ten, how much is your joy anchored in circumstances? Discuss.**

❶ ❷ ❸ ❹ ❺ ❻ ❼ ❽ ❾ ❿

My joy is not anchored in circumstances at all.

My joy is completely anchored in my circumstances.

3. **Take turns briefly describing a difficult season when you experienced the grace and peace from God that Paul describes.**

Lori vulnerably describes a battle with depression in which her therapist challenged her to do something every single day that brought her joy. She started with a walk, talking with others, avocado toast, and time with Jesus. Slowly God turned the lights back on in her life.

4. Select a few volunteers to split reading the passage Philippians 1:9–11. Discuss the following questions regarding the passage:

What is the focus of Paul's prayer?

When you pray, do you tend to focus more on your current circumstances or Christ?

How does this passage challenge you to shift your focus in your prayers?

Lori vulnerably describes a battle with depression in which her therapist challenged her to do something every single day that brought her joy. She started with a walk, talking with others, avocado toast, and time with Jesus. Slowly, God turned the lights back on in her life.

5. Go around the group and discuss the following questions:

When you're struggling with feeling down or discouraged, what simple acts spark joy in you?

When you notice someone falling into a dark or discouraged space, what is something you can do to call joy out again?

6. Are there any verses you go to in Scripture for a reminder of God's intention for our joy? Share with the group.

Close in Prayer

Consider the following prompts as you pray together for:

- Eyes to see where we're chasing happy instead of Jesus

- Opportunities to spark joy in ourselves and others

- God to turn the brightness all the way up

Preparation

To prepare for the next group session:

1. **Read Philippians 1:12–21.**

2. Tackle the three days of the Session One Personal Study.

3. Memorize this week's passage using the Beautiful Word Scripture memory coloring page. As a bonus, look up the Scripture memory passage in different translations and take note of the variations.

4. If you've agreed to bring something for the next session's Opening Group Activity, get it ready.

Joy isn't based on current **circumstances** but in the **character** of *God.*

IN ALL MY PRAYERS FOR ALL OF YOU,

I ALWAYS PRAY WITH JOY

PHILIPPIANS 1:4

SESSION
1

PERSONAL

STUDY TIME

DIGGING INTO THE

Beautiful WORD™
BIBLE STUDIES

PHILIPPIANS

CHASING JOY

DAY 1

ACTS 16—BACKGROUND OF PHILIPPIANS

Paul's letter to the Philippians is one of the most hopeful, joy-filled books of the Bible. Long before he penned this book, Paul spent time in Philippi, and everything we know about that visit is found in Acts 16.

Paul received a vision from the Lord that he was supposed to go to preach the gospel in Macedonia. So, Paul and his companions (Silas, Timothy, and Luke), hop in a boat and find their way to Philippi, a Roman colony and leading city in the area.

1. **Read Acts 16:6–10. How did God lead and direct Paul where to go?**

2. **Which patterns or methods have you noticed God uses to lead and direct you where He wants you to go? Circle any that apply.**

Scripture	Wise counsel
The Holy Spirit	Confirming situations
Other believers	Common sense
Still, quiet voice	Journaling
Creation	Specific circumstances
Overwhelming peace	Other _____

Paul,

whose original name was

Saul,

was likely named by his Jewish father after the first king of Israel.

There probably weren't enough Jewish men in Philippi to constitute a synagogue, so Paul and his buddies headed out to the river at the city gate where they expected to find a place of prayer. A group of women gathered there, and Paul was ready to start sharing the Good News of Jesus with them. The Bible says that the Lord opened the heart of a woman named Lydia to respond to Paul's message. Then Lydia and her whole household were baptized.

3. **Read Acts 16:16–18. How did the girl who was a slave respond to Paul and Silas?**

How did Paul respond to the girl who was a slave?

4. **How did the Spirit of God work in power through Paul?**

No wonder Paul thinks back on his time with the Philippians fondly and with joy. People were meeting Jesus and getting baptized. A girl was being set free from a demon. Lives were being changed!

But not everyone was happy about what was going on. The owners of that slave girl realized their money-making days were over, and they were furious. They hauled Paul and Silas before the city magistrates who ordered them to be stripped, severely beaten with rods, and thrown into prison. Jewish legal tradition of the time set a maximum number of blows that could be delivered when beating someone, but the Romans didn't have a limit. The beatings were ruthless. Bruised, broken, and humiliated, Paul and Silas were imprisoned in chains.

"When you feel weak and powerless, dry and lifeless, you can cling to

joy

because the power of the

Holy Spirit

is at work in you."

—Lori

5. **Read Acts 16:25.** How do Paul and Silas express joy that goes beyond their circumstances?

When have you faced a hardship and risen above in joy?

A huge earthquake struck, the prison cell doors flew open, and the chains came loose. God used that moment to let Paul and Silas introduce a jailer and his whole family to Jesus.

6. **Read Acts 16:40.** How do Paul and Silas conclude their time in Philippi?

While imprisoned in Philippi, Paul demonstrated that our joy doesn't need to be anchored to life's circumstances. Joy isn't based in our current circumstances; it's based in the character of God.

When you feel like you're walking through challenges and hardships alone, you can chase joy because God is with you.

DAY 2

PHILIPPIANS 1:1–4

Every book of the Bible differs in its beauty. Some books, like Psalms, consist of poetry. Other books, like the Gospels, focus on the life of Jesus. Philippians is what we call an "epistle," meaning a letter, written to the church in Philippi.

Paul wrote letters to keep in touch with congregations he had visited before moving on in his missionary journeys. In his letter to the Philippians, Paul recalls his amazing visit, and now that he is absent, he wants to return. Whether Paul is there or not, he wants his readers to know that they are in it together because of the good news of Jesus.

Like many of his other letters, Paul uses a three-part salutation: signature, address, and greeting. For us today, it may seem strange to begin with *who* wrote the letter before identifying the recipient, but that was common in Paul's time.

As you'll notice from the very first words of Paul's letter, though he has every reason to complain and be frustrated by his current imprisonment in Rome, instead he rallies in joy and celebration for the believers in Philippi.

1. **Read Philippians 1:1. Who is the letter written from, and who is the letter written to?**

   How are Paul and Timothy described?

   How are the believers in Philippi described?

   When you think of believers in Jesus, do you think of them in these terms? Why or why not?

In

PHILIPPIANS
1:1,

"holy people"

means

those who are
set apart.

Notice that Paul
writes to all the
holy people,
not just those
who have titles
or leadership
positions.

One common greeting in Greek was the *cherein*, which means greetings. Here Paul uses the Greek word *charis*, meaning unmerited favor. Paul combines this with the common Jewish greeting of "peace" which, in Hebrew, is *shalom*, and suggests a whole and full well-being in life.

2. **Read Philippians 1:2. In your life, where do you most need to experience grace and peace? Write a prayer in the space below.**

3. Read **Philippians 1:3–5**. What phrases does Paul use to describe his prayers? What phrases would you use to describe your prayers?

4. When it comes to prayer, what brings you the most joy? What brings you the least amount of joy?

5. Who is someone that you thank God for every time you think of that person (v. 3)?

6. Write a prayer of thanks for that person, then reach out and let the person know how much you celebrate them.

"Happiness will be ours, joyfulness will be found, delight will be experienced, gladness will be within our reach when we chase God's joy, His purpose, His encouragement, and His peace. Happy is captured when we chase Him."

— Lori

PHILIPPIANS 1:6-21

Paul teaches us that something mysterious and miraculous is happening. God is at work in His people, turning us from our old, selfish sinful nature so that we love what He loves. He is reworking our thoughts and healing the wounds of our hearts. He is taking what was dead and bringing life once again. He is shifting us from sin to salvation.

1. **Read Philippians 1:6.** On the continuum below, how easy or hard is it for you to believe this for your own life?

❶ ❷ ❸ ❹ ❺ ❻ ❼ ❽ ❾ ❿

I struggle to believe this promise for my life.　　It's easy to believe this promise for my life.

On the next continuum, how easy or hard is it for you to believe this promise for other people's lives?

❶ ❷ ❸ ❹ ❺ ❻ ❼ ❽ ❾ ❿

I struggle to believe this promise for other people's lives.　　It's easy to believe this promise for other people's lives.

If your answers differed on the continuums, why do you think that is?

2. How could clinging to this promise change the way you live or respond to situations?

3. Read **Philippians 1:7–8**. What are three practical ways you can show love with the "affection of Jesus Christ" (v. 8)?

   1. _____

   2. _____

   3. _____

Paul shares a beautiful prayer of joy for the Philippians. Notice that this joyful prayer isn't about their current circumstance; it's about Christ. God's love flowed into them and through them as they partnered with Paul in his work to spread the Good News, which causes him to experience joy. When we let God's love move in us, through us, and to others, we aren't the only ones who will experience joy. That joy spreads to those around us.

4. Read **Philippians 1:9–11**. What is the result of God's love having its full effect?

Paul doesn't just pray that we will be filled until we are overflowing with agape love; he also prays that we will be filled with the fruit of righteousness—or right living—that comes through Jesus (v. 11). The fruits of righteousness are the evidence of God's saving work in us and the effects of it springing from our renewed hearts.

5. What role do each of the following play in your spiritual life? Fill in the chart below. Then take a moment to pray **Philippians 1:9–11** over yourself and someone you love.

ELEMENT OF PAUL'S PRAYER	SCRIPTURE	ROLE IN YOUR SPIRITUAL LIFE
Abounding in Love	Philippians **1:9**	
Knowledge and Depth of Insight	Philippians **1:9**	
Discern What's Best	Philippians **1:10**	

ELEMENT OF PAUL'S PRAYER	SCRIPTURE	ROLE IN YOUR SPIRITUAL LIFE
Live Pure and Blameless	Philippians **1:10**	
Filled with the Fruit of Righteousness	Philippians **1:11**	

6. Read **Philippians 1:12–21** to prepare for the next session. Summarize what happens in this passage in two to three sentences.

"BECAUSE IT IS *God,* NOT US, WHO BEGAN THAT GOOD WORK, WE CAN BE *confident* THAT HE WILL SEE IT THROUGH."

—LORI

Reflection

As you reflect on your personal study of **Philippians 1:1–21**,
what are the BEAUTIFUL WORDS the Holy Spirit
has been highlighting to you through this time?
Write or draw them in the space below:

CHASING
PURPOSE

PHILIPPIANS

Opening Group Activity (10-15 MINUTES)

WHAT YOU WILL NEED:

* A list of five to eight questions that ask, "What's your favorite . . . ?"

1. Make a list of questions that ask, "What's your favorite _____?" or use the following list: What's your favorite food? Snack? Restaurant? Season? Holiday? Sports team? Way to spend an afternoon? Time to wake up?

2. Invite participants to share their favorites and get to know each other better.

    What do you think shapes your preferences in life?

    How do you tend to respond when you don't get what you prefer?

Watch Session Two Video (23 MINUTES)

Group leader, stream the video or play the DVD.

As you watch, take notes while thinking through:

What caught your attention? • • • • • • • • • • • • • ➤

What surprised you? • • • • • • • • • • • • • • ➤

What made you reflect? • • • • • • • • • • • • ➤

One of God's purposes is that the Good News is shared.

Disappointments can be God appointments.

Your trouble is your testimony.

The Good News of Jesus went out—the goodness of God was proclaimed.

God is working *in* our difficulty.

We find happy in God's purpose.

SCRIPTURE COVERED IN THIS SESSION:
PHILIPPIANS 1:12-21

Group Discussion Questions (30-45 MINUTES)

Group leader, read each numbered prompt and question to the group and select volunteers for Scripture reading.

• • • • •

"We all have **preferences** in life. We'd **prefer** life to go a certain way. We'd **prefer** what we want, when we want it. We'd **prefer** that our prayers were answered the way we envisioned in the timing we imagined. But our **preferences** aren't as important as **God's purpose**." — Lori

• • • • •

When it comes to your workplace, family, or relationships, where do you find your preferences leaving you feeling frustrated or overwhelmed?

How can reorienting your focus toward God and His purpose bring clarity?

1. **Select a volunteer to read the passage Philippians 1:12–14. Describe a time when something felt like a big disappointment but was really a God appointment.**

Lori shares the story of hearing the words from Jud's mentor, "Your **wife** will **make** or **break** you in **ministry**." She was **horrified** by the thought that she could cause her husband's ministry to **fail** and was overcome by **insecurity** and **discouragement**. Yet it's from this place of **pain** she started **Leading** and **Loving** It to **encourage** other women in ministry. Though she wouldn't venture back through that dark time again, as she stepped out of her **preference** and into God's **purpose**, she discovered so much **joy**.

2. **When has God turned your hurt into an opportunity for healing for others?**

3. **Are there any areas of previous pain that you'd like to see God use to bring healing and hope to others?**

4. **Select two volunteers to take turns reading the passage Philippians 1:15–19. Discuss the following:**

    Where do you wrestle with a spirit of competition with coworkers, friends, or family?

    What would it look like for you to find great joy in all God does in and through His people?

"Paul knows there're just **two** options. He would either be delivered from this situation through an **extended life** on earth or delivered in the midst of his **situation through life** forever with Jesus. Either way, he **rejoiced** because, in life or death, Jesus would be **exalted**. Sometimes we can be **tempted** to believe that if we weren't delivered from our **difficulty**, then God must not have been working in our **difficulty**. But often **deliverance** comes in the midst of our situations by the **giving** of Himself." — Lori

5. Go around the group and discuss the following questions:

When has God delivered you in the midst of a life challenge?

What did you learn from that experience?

6. How were you able to rejoice in Christ because of that?

Where in your life do you need to step out of your preference and into God's purpose?

Close in Prayer

Consider the following prompts as you pray together for:

- Releasing preferences to lay hold of God's purpose

- Eyes to see how God is working in your difficulties

- New joy as you chase Him

Preparation

To prepare for the next group session:

1. **Read Philippians 2:1–11.**

2. Tackle the three days of the Session Two Personal Study.

3. Memorize this week's passage using the Beautiful Word Scripture memory coloring page. As a bonus, look up the Scripture memory passage in different translations and take note of the variations.

4. If you've agreed to bring something for the next session's Opening Group Activity, get it ready.

It's time to step out of your preference and into God's purpose.

THE IMPORTANT THING IS THAT IN EVERY WAY, WHETHER FROM FALSE MOTIVES OR TRUE, CHRIST IS PREACHED. AND BECAUSE OF THIS I REJOICE.

YES, AND I WILL CONTINUE TO REJOICE.

PHILIPPIANS 1:18

SESSION

2

PERSONAL STUDY TIME

DIGGING INTO THE

Beautiful WORD™

BIBLE STUDIES

PHILIPPIANS

CHASING PURPOSE

PHILIPPIANS 1:12-18

Our preferences aren't as important as God's purpose. Paul reminds us that God's purposes are that Christ is preached and that the Good News is shared. Paul teaches us that the method and the motive don't really matter. It's the message of Christ going forward that really matters.

Paul had hoped to come to Rome as a powerful preacher. He was ready to share the life-changing grace and mercy of Jesus with the people there. Instead, he entered Rome as a suppressed prisoner, or at least that was the goal of those who arrested him. The final verse of the book of Acts says for two years Paul "proclaimed the kingdom of God and taught about the Lord Jesus Christ—with all boldness and without hinderance" (Acts 28:31).

Paul wasn't suppressed and the message of Christ wasn't hindered. No earthly chains could hold back the heavenly good news.

1. Read **Philippians 1:12–14**. In the box below, draw a picture of Paul in chains.

"For this reason I have asked to see you and talk with you. It is because of the hope of Israel that I am bound with this chain.

Acts 28:20

How did Paul's chains position him to declare the Gospel?

2. What was the surprising impact of Paul's chains on other believers? (Hint: v. 14)

3. When has your or someone else's suffering resulted in the message of Christ being proclaimed?

4. In the space below, draw a picture of some of the "chains" you're wearing—things that you feel are holding you back.

How could Jesus be using these chains to position you for His greater purpose?

Some people, motivated by a spirit of competition and envy, sought to take advantage of the fact that Paul was sidelined by his imprisonment. They saw an opportunity to gain more and more influence and build a larger ministry than Paul. They were driven by a discontentment that sprang up when they saw Paul's achievements, and they wanted that for themselves. They didn't just want to come out as winners; they wanted Paul to lose. Those preachers couldn't understand that Paul simply didn't care. He sure wasn't going to let their motives steal his joy.

5. Read **Philippians 1:15–18**. What are some modern ways Christ can be proclaimed out of rivalry, selfish motives, or greed?

How does Paul's response to insincere teachers equip you to respond to those who are insincere?

6. Where have you experienced malicious people making your life more difficult?

How can you respond more like Paul?

"Paul didn't care about the method or motive. He only cared that the message of the Good News of Jesus went out and the goodness of God was proclaimed."

—Lori

> "However, if you suffer as a Christian, do not be ashamed, but praise God that you bear that name."
>
> **1 Peter 4:16**

DAY 2

PHILIPPIANS 1:19-26

Paul knew things weren't looking great for him. While he was in prison, he was awaiting trial before the Roman emperor Nero who, as we know from history, was not a fan of Christians. He threw Christians into gladiator matches and fed them to lions. It's said that he lit his garden parties using the burning remains of Christians as torches. Yet it's in this place—literally between a rock and a hard place—that Paul demonstrates an unwavering faith.

1. Read **Philippians 1:19** and reflect on the areas of life where you need to make this powerful declaration. Then, fill in the blanks identifying them and personalizing Paul's words. Lastly, read each declaration aloud.

   Example: "For I know that through your prayers and God's provision of the Spirit of Jesus Christ, _the loss of my job_ will turn out for my deliverance."

   "For I know that through your prayers and God's provision of the Spirit of Jesus Christ, _____

   _____ will turn out for my deliverance."

   "For I know that through your prayers and God's provision of the Spirit of Jesus Christ, _____

   _____ will turn out for my deliverance."

   "For I know that through your prayers and God's provision of the Spirit of Jesus Christ, _____

   _____ will turn out for my deliverance."

"For I know that through your prayers and God's provision of the Spirit of Jesus Christ, _____

_____

will turn out for my deliverance."

"For I know that through your prayers and God's provision of the Spirit of Jesus Christ, _____

_____

will turn out for my deliverance."

Paul knows there are just two options. He would either be delivered from this situation through an extended life on earth or delivered amid his situation through life forever with Jesus. Either way, he rejoiced because, in life or death, Jesus would be exalted.

2. Read **Philippians 1:20**. **Reflecting on personal hardships, in what ways is your happiness or contentment dependent on a particular outcome rather than on Christ?**

3. **List three areas where you need to step out of your preferences and into God's purposes. Circle the one that's the easiest and underline the one that's most challenging.**

Out of preferences • • • . . . ➤ Into God's purposes

1.

2.

3.

All these people were still living by faith when they died. They did not receive the things promised; they only saw them and welcomed them from a distance, admitting that they were foreigners and strangers on earth.

Hebrews 11:13

4. Read **Philippians 1:21–26** and, reflecting on the passage, fill in the chart below.

QUESTION	PERSONAL RESPONSE
How can Christ be exalted in your life?	
How can Christ be exalted even through death?	
What does it mean to you that to live is Christ and to die is gain?	

5. How does Paul's perspective free you to live less attached to the things of this world and more attached to Jesus?

6. How does Paul's perspective help you to wait well when you don't know the future?

God exalted him to his own right hand as Prince and Savior that he might bring Israel to repentance and forgive their sins.

Acts 5:31

DAY 3

PHILIPPIANS 1:27–2:11

Paul concludes this opening chapter by calling readers to live a life that's worthy of the Gospel. He wants believers not just to hear God's Word but to live out God's Word in such a way the world will take notice.

1. Read **Philippians 1:27–28**. What does it look like for you to conduct yourself in a manner worthy of Jesus?

2. What's one way in which your conduct is not worthy of the Gospel right now?

What changes do you need to make so that it is worthy of the Gospel?

"Clinging too tightly to your personal preferences will eventually hold you back from God's greater purposes."
—Lori

Paul calls believers to unity, but that doesn't mean uniformity or thinking and doing the exact same things. Rather, Paul calls believers to make Jesus the center of a loving Christian community.

3. **Where do you see believers struggling with unity most right now?**

What personal preferences do you need to let go of to lean into God's higher purpose of unity among believers?

4. **Read Philippians 1:29–30. What role has suffering played in your faith journey?**

5. **Has your suffering caused you to doubt or second-guess God and following Jesus? If so, describe.**

6. How has your suffering caused you to deepen your faith and trust of God?

7. Read **Philippians 2:1–11** to prepare for the next session. Summarize what happens in this passage in two to three sentences.

Reflection

As you reflect on your personal study of **Philippians 1:12—2:11**, what are the BEAUTIFUL WORDS the Holy Spirit has been highlighting to you through this time? Write or draw them in the space below:

SESSION
3

CHASING
UNITY

PHILIPPIANS

Opening Group Activity (10-15 MINUTES)

WHAT YOU WILL NEED:

* A long piece of thin rope or string (measure it to be as long as needed with an estimation of about three feet long per person)

* Note: if you have a larger group, keep each thin rope or string to a maximum of twenty four feet per group and each group to a maximum of eight people for this activity.

1. Tie the thin rope or string together at the ends. Then have each group—up to eight people—form a circle around it.

2. Invite each person to grab the thin rope or string with both hands at waist height.

3. Ask each group to work together to form the following shapes: circle, square, rectangle, diamond, star, and figure eight.

4. If you have multiple groups, consider making it a game to see which group can finish the fastest.

5. Discuss the following questions:

   What was the biggest challenge in working together to form the shapes?

   How did working together help to form the shapes?

   On a scale of one to ten, how important was unity in accomplishing the tasks? Explain.

Watch Session Three Video (23 MINUTES)

Group leader, stream the video or play the DVD.

As you watch, take notes while thinking through:

What caught your attention? • • • • • • • • • • • • • • ➤

What surprised you? • • • • • • • • • • • • • • • • ➤

What made you reflect? • • • • • • • • • • • • • ➤

Happiness is unity with Christ and others.

....

Encouragement is renewing, strengthening, and lifting up the hearts of
    God's people.

....

Comfort = come close and speak tenderly

....

Circle of compassion

....

Take in Jesus' tender mercy and compassion; then give it to others.

....

Humility is the mindset of Christ.

....

SCRIPTURE COVERED IN THIS SESSION:
PHILIPPIANS 2:1-11

Group Discussion Questions (30-45 MINUTES)

Group leader, read each numbered prompt and question to the group and select volunteers for Scripture reading.

• • • • •

"Thankfully, the **connection** between believers isn't something that will make you cringe, cry, or steal your joy. That's because **unity** isn't based on a thing, it's based on the **person** of Jesus Christ. Being unified with Christ **empowers** us to be unified with others. And that will bring you **joy.**" — Lori

• • • • •

How would you have responded if you were given the same gift Lori describes?

What does it mean for you to be unified with other believers?

What's been your greatest experience of unity with other believers?

Where would you most like to experience unity with other believers?

1. **Ask a volunteer to read Philippians 2:1–4 and invite participants to respond to the following:**

   What are the four "If's" Paul lists and how have you experienced each of these "Ifs"?

2. **Select a few volunteers to split reading the passage Philippians 2:5–11. Discuss some of the following questions:**

   What does it look like for you to humble yourself before God and others?

   What's one relationship in which arrogance has been getting the best of you?

   What can you do to bring healing to this relationship?

   • • • • •

   "**Humility** in our relationships is taking the time to really **listen** to others even though you have lots of **unchecked** items on your to-do list. Humility is **seeking** wisdom and **feedback** from other leaders so you can grow. It's **owning** your **mistakes** instead of **running** away from them and seeking forgiveness when **needed**. Humility is showing **appreciation** for others, not just for what they do, but for **who** they are." — Lori

   • • • • •

Unity with **CHRIST** *leads to unity with* **OTHERS.**

3. **Lori offers four practical ways to demonstrate humility and chase unity. Which of these comes easiest for you and which is most challenging?**

What is one more practical way you can demonstrate humility and chase unity?

Lori describes visiting a group of believers in Romania who had opened their doors to those in need.

4. **What inspired you most about Lori's story?**

5. **How have you found compassion to be a circle in which, as you receive Jesus' compassion, you're empowered to extend it to others?**

6. **How does unity with Christ lead to unity with others in your life?**

Close in Prayer

Consider the following prompts as you pray together for:

- A fresh desire to pursue unity with Christ
- Courage to chase unity with others
- Opportunities to do things for the good of others and the glory of God

Preparation

To prepare for the next group session:

1. **Read Philippians 2:1–3:21.**

2. Tackle the three days of the Session Three Personal Study.

3. Memorize this week's passage using the Beautiful Word Scripture memory coloring page. As a bonus, look up the Scripture memory passage in different translations and take note of the variations.

4. If you've agreed to bring something for the next session's Opening Group Activity, get it ready.

MAKE MY JOY COMPLETE
BY BEING LIKE-MINDED, HAVING THE SAME LOVE,
BEING ONE IN SPIRIT AND OF ONE MIND.

PHILIPPIANS 2:2

SESSION
3

PERSONAL
STUDY TIME

DIGGING INTO THE

PHILIPPIANS
CHASING UNITY

The Latin root words for "encouragement" are in and heart—meaning to

inspire

someone's heart with confidence, hope, and strength.

DAY 1

PHILIPPIANS 2:1-11

At the end of the first chapter of Philippians, Paul encourages believers to walk in a manner that's worthy of the Gospel—in a way that demonstrates the beauty and power of being a Christ-follower. That worthy calling is spelled out in specific ways beginning in chapter two.

Many modern translations use the word "if," suggesting that _if_ the readers have encountered Christ, His comfort, and His spirit, _then_—as some translations say—Paul's joy will be complete, by being in unity with one another. After all, unity with Christ can lead you to unity with others.

But in the original Greek, Paul wasn't asking _if_ the people of Philippi had experienced these things, or even doubting that they had. Rather, Paul genuinely knew they'd experienced the presence of Christ in their faith and life. Another way to read the four clauses in Philippians 2:1 is by replacing _if_ with _since_.

1. Read **Philippians 2:1. In the space below, rewrite the verse replacing** _if_ with _since_.

How does Paul affirm the believers and their relationship with Jesus?

2. Read **Philippians 2:2–4**. Which of the following best describes being of the same mind according to Paul? Circle all that apply.

> Thinking the exact same way
>
> Putting others above yourself
>
> Having a common attitude toward Christ and others
>
> Agreeing 100 percent on everything
>
> Serving one another
>
> Sharing a similar mindset

3. What are three downsides of only surrounding yourself with people who think, believe, and see the world just like you?

    • _____
       _____

    • _____
       _____

    • _____
       _____

4. What are two ways believers who have different perspectives on faith can still practice being of the same mind?

    • _____
       _____

    • _____
       _____

How have you worked to lovingly overcome intense differences with other believers?

"Want to make your joy complete? Want to chase happy? Then chase unity. Being unified with Christ empowers us to be unified with others. Our unity with Christ leads us to unity with others. The same love. The same spirit. The same mind."

—Lori

The Bible says that Jesus made Himself nothing. A more common way to translate that phrase would be "He emptied Himself." Jesus didn't empty Himself of His deity, His divine attributes, or His equality with God. He was still fully God. But He did empty Himself into the form of a servant. The original language Paul uses here isn't saying that Jesus is making an exchange of His divinity for His humanity, but rather adding humanity to His already existing divinity. And He did that humbly.

5. Read **Philippians 2:5–8**. What are some ways we behave and have a mindset that's opposite of Christ?

When have you seen someone use their relationship with God for their own advantage (v. 6)?

When have you seen someone try to make themselves something special to gain power and prestige (v. 7)?

When have you seen someone behave arrogantly or unruly, as if the rules didn't apply to them (v. 8)?

Through Jesus' obedience, sacrifice, humility, and servanthood, in heaven and on earth, the fullness of creation will acknowledge that Jesus is Lord to the glory of God.

6. **Read Philippians 2:9–11. How do you think the church today would look different if every believer had the mindset of Christ?**

What changes do you need to make to take on the mindset of Christ today? Write your answer in the space below.

The verb "work out" in Greek means to "continually engage in the effort to bring something to completion or fruition."

DAY 2

PHILIPPIANS 2:12-18

Whenever you see the word "therefore" in the Bible, it's worth asking, *what's it there for?* As Paul continues his letter, he is building on the encouragement that he started in 1:27. Whether Paul is present or absent from the Philippians, they are to live out their faith in obedience and joy. Paul challenges that following Jesus is more than just what's in our heads—it's what's in our hearts, hands, and actions.

1. Read **Philippians 2:12–13**. On the continuum below, mark whether you're working more for your salvation or working out your salvation right now.

I'm working
for my
salvation.

I'm working
out my
salvation.

What is the difference between working *for* your salvation and working *out* your salvation?

Which results in more happiness and joy? Explain.

Throughout the Old Testament, a common response to God's presence was fear and trembling. Some people have used Philippians 2:12 to suggest that people should somehow live in anxiety of God. But the word used for "fear" in Greek can also be translated as respect or reverence.

2. **Look up the following passages and fill in the chart below noting what each passage reveals about reverence to God.**

PASSAGE	RESPONSE TO GOD
Deuteronomy **10:12**	
Joshua **24:14**	
Psalm **2:11**	
Isaiah **50:10**	
1 Corinthians **2:3**	

3. How has obedience and dependence on God empowered you to experience more happiness and joy?

Paul calls believers to maturity and says the fruit of their lives will be demonstrated in how they respond to God and others.

4. Read **Philippians 2:14–16.** On the continuum below, how much do you struggle with complaining or grumbling?

❶ ❷ ❸ ❹ ❺ ❻ ❼ ❽ ❾ ❿

I struggle with complaining.

I never complain.

On the next continuum, how much do you struggle with picking a fight or arguing with others?

❶ ❷ ❸ ❹ ❺ ❻ ❼ ❽ ❾ ❿

I struggle with picking fights or arguing with others.

I never struggle with picking fights nor arguing with others.

Are you more tempted by grumbling or arguing? Explain.

5. How have you seen grumbling and arguing create disunity among believers?

In Philippians 2:15, what promise does Paul give for those who resist grumbling and arguing and hold firmly to God's Word?

6. Read **Philippians 2:17–18**. In the space below, draw a picture of the ways you are being poured out like a drink offering for the love and service of God and others.

How is this pouring out bringing you happiness and joy?

DAY 3

PHILIPPIANS 2:19-3:21

Moving through life without deep, meaningful friendship is hard. Paul knows this firsthand. One of his best friends in ministry was Timothy, who had been a companion and encouragement to Paul for years. Timothy delivered reports to Paul regarding various churches (1 Thessalonians 3:6) and served as Paul's spokesperson in 1 and 2 Timothy.

1. Read **Philippians 2:19–24. Make a list of the qualities of Timothy. Which do you desire for your life the most?**

   Who is someone in your life who shares some of the same qualities as Timothy?

2. **When have you had a relationship with someone like that of Paul and Timothy?**

For this reason I have sent to you Timothy, my son whom I love, who is faithful in the Lord. He will remind you of my way of life in Christ Jesus, which agrees with what I teach everywhere in every church.

1 Corinthians 4:17

How did that relationship bring you the right kind of happiness?

Paul also mentions Epaphroditus, who is not mentioned in the Bible outside of Philippians. His name suggests he was not a Jew, and Paul describes him as the one who delivered the gifts from the church at Philippi to Paul.

3. Read **Philippians 2:25–30**. What are the great qualities of Epaphroditus?

How does Paul demonstrate in this passage that he's more concerned for the church of Philippi, Timothy, and Epaphroditus than himself?

4. Paul esteems Timothy and Epaphroditus without putting them on a pedestal. How can you esteem fellow believers without putting them on a pedestal?

> *Greater love has no one than* THIS: *to lay down one's life for one's friends.*
>
> **John 15:13**

5. If spiritual leaders were to describe you, which words do you think they'd use? Circle all that apply.

Kind	Loving	Patient	Gracious
Thoughtful	Tender	Humble	Strategic
Resilient	Dedicated	Loyal	Joyful
Insightful	Happy	Disciplined	Content

6. **Read Philippians 3 to prepare for the next session. Summarize what happens in this passage in two to three sentences.**

Reflection

As you reflect on your personal study of **Philippians 2:1—3:21,**
what are the BEAUTIFUL WORDS the Holy Spirit
has been highlighting to you through this time?
Write or draw them in the space below:

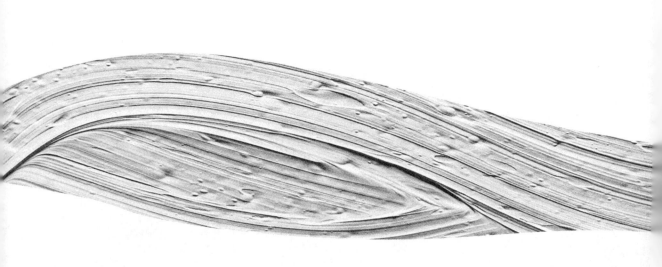

SESSION
4

CHASING
CHRIST

PHILIPPIANS

Opening Group Activity (10-15 MINUTES)

WHAT YOU WILL NEED:

* Photocopies of the Get to Know You Even Better worksheet on page 145 of this study guide.

* Pens

    1. Invite each person to fill out the Get to Know You Even Better worksheet.

    2. Take turns sharing each person's answers.

Watch Session Four Video (22 MINUTES)

Group leader, stream the video or play the DVD.

As you watch, take notes while thinking through:

What caught your attention? • • • • • • • • • • • • • • ➤

What surprised you? • • • • • • • • • • • • • • • ➤

What made you reflect? • • • • • • • • • • • • • ➤

Be continually rejoicing.

Ritual can replace relationship and steal your happy.

Rejoicing is cultivated in our connection with Christ.

Gaining Christ and being found by Him—life floods with joy!

Get to *know* Christ. Don't just know *about* Him.

SCRIPTURE COVERED IN THIS SESSION:
PHILIPPIANS 3:1-14

Group Discussion Questions (30-45 MINUTES)

Group leader, read each numbered prompt and question to the group and select volunteers for Scripture reading.

• • • • •

Paul says—**Listen**! I know I've said it a bunch of times. Be **joyful**. Be **glad**. Be **happy**. But I'm just going to keep on saying it because it's good for you to hear. It should be on **repeat** in your minds. And it will **safeguard** your faith. So, here it is again: **Rejoice** in the Lord. This isn't a one-time thing—go on **constantly** rejoicing. — Lori

• • • • •

What's an area of life where you have no interest whatsoever in rejoicing?

What does it look like for you to rejoice in the Lord, even when you can't rejoice in the circumstances?

How does rejoicing act as a safeguard to negativity and fear (Philippians 3:1)?

1. **Invite several volunteers to take turns reading through 2 Corinthians 11:23–30, and respond to some of the following:**

   How was Paul able to rejoice not just in times of blessing but in times of suffering, too?

   What helps you cling to Christ and find joy in difficult seasons?

2. **Select a few volunteers to split reading the passage Philippians 3:4–9. Discuss some of the following questions:**

   What religious credentials does Paul list?

   What would you list as your modern religious credentials? (Examples: grew up in a Christian home, try to do the right things, attend church, join Bible studies, live as a go-getter for God)

   Where are you tempted to think that if you just do enough, earn enough, sacrifice enough, or fill-in-the-blank, then Jesus will love you more?

• • • • •

"Maybe you've **given** your **heart** to Jesus recently. But that fiery passion you had in the beginning has begun to **cool** off. Or maybe you've been **walking** with God for years or even decades. But, if you're **honest**, your spiritual life feels **dry** and **lifeless**. Or maybe you've never **trusted** Jesus with your life. You know God's been **tapping** you on the shoulder, trying to snag your **attention**. It's time to receive a **relationship** with Jesus. **Rediscovering** a relationship with Jesus leads to rediscovering joy." — Lori

• • • • •

3. **What one adjective best describes your relationship with Jesus right now?**

   Which of the following do you most need to experience: a fresh awareness of His mercy, an added experience of His forgiveness, or an extra depth in knowing Him? Discuss.

4. **How does knowing and experiencing Jesus spark joy in you?**

5. **Go around the group discussing a selection of the following questions:**

   Are there any special places or practices that ignite your love for Jesus?

What stops you from going there or engaging in those practices?

What would it look like for you to chase Jesus above all else this week?

Close in Prayer

Consider the following prompts as you pray together for:

- A fresh understanding of grace and mercy
- A personal and meaningful encounter with Jesus
- Rekindled passion for Christ

Preparation

To prepare for the next group session:

1. Read Philippians 3:1–4:9.
2. Tackle the three days of the Session Four Personal Study.
3. Memorize this week's passage using the Beautiful Word Scripture memory coloring page. As a bonus, look up the Scripture memory passage in different translations and take note of the variations.
4. If you've agreed to bring something for the next session's Opening Group Activity, get it ready.

Rediscovering a relationship with Jesus leads to rediscovering joy.

FURTHER, MY BROTHERS AND SISTERS, REJOICE IN THE LORD!

PHILIPPIANS 3:1

PERSONAL STUDY TIME

DIGGING INTO THE

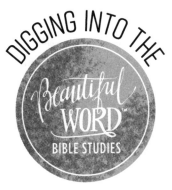

Beautiful WORD™ BIBLE STUDIES

PHILIPPIANS

CHASING CHRIST

DAY 1

PHILIPPIANS 3:1–7

Paul had multiple run-ins with a group of people called the Judaizers who were Jewish Christians that followed Paul around. As he would lead Gentiles to Christ, they would come in behind him and tell the people that they couldn't be made right with God until they were circumcised and followed the law of Moses.

Now, the law of Moses was more than just the Ten Commandments. It was the set of laws found in the first five books of the Old Testament. It was the perfect standard by which people were supposed to conduct their lives. There was just one problem: People aren't perfect. So, the law of Moses revealed the imperfection in people and showed that they could not fulfill the law on their own. They needed a savior.

The Judaizers believed salvation hinged not just on a relationship with Christ, but also on circumcision, a ritual that must be done. Paul, the apostle Peter, and the early church leaders met together to discuss the beliefs and teachings of the Judaizers in Acts 15.

1. Read **Acts 15:1–11.** What does Peter say is the true source of salvation?

2. Read **Philippians 3:1–3.** Why is Paul so angry against false teachers who put confidence in the flesh?

We believe it is through the grace of our Lord Jesus that we are saved, just as they are.

Acts 15:11

In your life, in which types of things are you tempted to place confidence? Circle all that apply.

Social media influence   Sports skills

Family name or history   Special talents

Finances   Professional accomplishments

Social status   Popularity

Children's successes   Other_____

3. Read **Philippians 3:4–7. What is most important in life for Paul?**

4. **What is most important in your life?**

5. **What are three ways in which you can boast or take great joy and delight in Christ now?**

- _____

- _____

- _____

> "Rejoicing is cultivated in our connection with Christ."
> —**Lori**

6. Write a prayer in the space below thanking Jesus for what He's done for you and the work He has done in you.

_____

_____

_____

_____

_____

_____

_____

_____

_____

_____

_____

_____

_____

_____

_____

_____

_____

_____

_____

_____

_____

_____

_____

_____

DAY 2

PHILIPPIANS 3:8-11

If anyone could brag about his religious credentials, it was Paul. He was circumcised on the eighth day in accordance with Leviticus 12:3. He was an Israelite, one of God's chosen people, and an heir to the promise of God to His people. He was part of the tribe of Benjamin, a distinguished and loyal tribe.

Paul was a Hebrew of Hebrews—a Hebrew man, raised by Hebrew parents, and proud of his Hebrew heritage. He was a Pharisee, part of the religious elite, dedicated to keeping every detail of the law in his life. And he was zealous. He was so dedicated to God that he persecuted Christians who he believed were the opponents of Judaism before he met Jesus himself. Yet he declares all these credentials were nothing compared to knowing Christ!

1. Read **Philippians 3:8–9** and write the passage in your own words.

What challenges you most from Paul's declaration?

2. What are three things that used to be important to you that you now see as rubbish compared to knowing Jesus?

- ● _____
  _____

- ● _____
  _____

- ● _____
  _____

3. What's something that used to make you happy that now feels empty because you know Jesus?

4. How has knowing Jesus disrupted your value system?

5. Sum up in one sentence what knowing and loving Jesus means to you.

Paul reminds us that we can rediscover friendship with Jesus. It may feel like a lot of life has happened since you last connected with Him. But you might be struck with how "the same" He is. Jesus wants you to know Him. Not just know about Him, but to truly know Him. To be in His presence and share day-to-day life with Him. With Jesus, nothing is off-limits.

6. Read **Philippians 3:10–11. How have you experienced the power of the resurrection in your life?**

How have you participated in the suffering of Christ?

DAY 3

PHILIPPIANS 3:12–4:9

Though Paul finds his contentment in Christ, he never settles when it comes to growing in Jesus. He knows he is in a spiritual race, and though he grows physically tired, he presses forward toward Jesus. Paul demonstrates what it looks like to chase Jesus with everything we've got.

1. **Read Philippians 3:12–14. On the continuum below, mark how much you feel stuck in your spiritual life.**

I feel stuck
in my
relationship
with God.

I feel like
I'm flourishing
in my
relationship
with God.

Are there any things from your past that you need to receive forgiveness for, heal from, and move on from? If so, describe.

In the space below, write a prayer asking Jesus to heal and restore you.

THEY
ARE NOT
OF THE
WORLD,
EVEN AS
I AM NOT
OF IT.
John 17:16

2. In what specific ways have you been maturing in Christ over the last year?

Does reflecting on the ways Christ is growing you encourage you to remain faithful? Why or why not?

3. Read **Philippians 3:15–20.** Do you tend to find your citizenship more in heaven or on earth? Explain.

How would your life be different if you thought of yourself as a citizen of heaven?

As Paul enters the final chapter of his letter, he encourages his readers to stand firm in Jesus. He encourages unity and peace among people in the church.

4. Read **Philippians 4:1. How does Paul describe his brothers and sisters of the faith?**

Name three people of deep faith whom you treasure and enjoy.

- _____
- _____
- _____

Take a moment to text, email, or call them and let them know!

Paul then mentions two women: Euodia and Syntyche. While we don't know much about them, we can guess they had likely worked directly with Paul when the church began and were now at odds with each other. The disruption in their relationship was likely spilling out to those around them.

5. Read **Philippians 4:2–3**. What does Paul prescribe for Euodia and Syntyche?

Fill in the chart below. In your life, who are believers with differing thoughts with whom you need to make peace? What strategy can you implement to restore peace?

BELIEVER YOU DISAGREE WITH	STRATEGY TO RESTORE PEACE

6. Read **Philippians 4:4–9** to prepare for the next session. **Summarize what happens in this passage in two to three sentences.**

Reflection

As you reflect on your personal study of **Philippians 3:1—4:9**,
what are the BEAUTIFUL WORDS the Holy Spirit
has been highlighting to you through this time?
Write or draw them in the space below:

SESSION
5

CHASING
PEACE

PHILIPPIANS

Opening Group Activity (10-15 MINUTES)

WHAT YOU WILL NEED:

* A music player (such as a smartphone) with a downloaded playlist so you are ready to play the song "Tomorrow" by Central Live.

* A printed or digital copy of the song lyrics

1. Listen and/or sing along to the selected song. As you listen, pay attention to what thoughts this worship song evokes.

2. Discuss the following questions:

   What do the lyrics of this song make you think about?

   How does listening or singing along with this song affect your emotions and perspective?

   How does focusing your mind on Jesus affect you in the everyday?

Watch Session Five Video (22 MINUTES)

Group leader, stream the video or play the DVD.

As you watch, take notes while thinking through:

What caught your attention? · · · · · · · · · · · · · · ·▶

What surprised you? · · · · · · · · · · · · · · · · ·▶

What made you reflect? · · · · · · · · · · · · · · ·▶

What continually runs through my mind will continually run through my life.

....

God is "the perfectly happy and only Ruler."

....

The pathway from panic to peace is prayer.

....

Turn your worst times into your worship times.

....

God's Word is perfect, trustworthy, right, radiant, pure, and righteous.

....

The peace of God in you. And the God of peace with you.

....

SCRIPTURE COVERED IN THIS SESSION:
PHILIPPIANS 4:4–9

Group Discussion Questions (30-45 MINUTES)

Group leader, read each numbered prompt and question to the group and select volunteers for Scripture reading.

• • • • •

> Lori shares that we have upwards of seventy thousand **thoughts** a day. Some are **constructive** like, "I did it!" or "I'm so proud of myself!" Others are **destructive** like, "I'm never going to amount to anything!" or "I'm not a good enough wife, mom, or friend!"

• • • • •

What influences tend to shape your thought life?

On a scale of one to ten, how harsh are you in the words you say about yourself?

Where do you think you learned this kind of thinking?

1. **Select volunteers to read the passages Philippians 4:4–7 and Matthew 6:25–27. Discuss the following:**

   In what areas of life do you tend to struggle with anxiety or worry the most?

   What do Paul and Jesus advise when it comes to anxiety and worry?

What have you found to be the most effective when it comes to breaking a cycle of anxiety and worry?

• • • • •

"The pathway from **panic** to **peace** is prayer. It's extremely difficult for the closed-fist posture of **worry**, **anxiety**, and **stress** to coexist with the hands-raised posture of **worship**. When we come to God with **open** hands, **acknowledging** His goodness, recognizing His kindness, **trusting** His sovereignty and control, we **release** the worry we've been holding onto so tightly." — Lori

• • • • •

2. **What roles do worship and prayer play in fixing your eyes on Jesus and taking control of your thought life?**

3. **Describe a time when you turned your worst time into a worship time. What was the result?**

4. **What's one difficult area where you need to worship anyway?**

Describe a time when you experienced the overwhelming peace of God. How did that experience reshape your perspective of the situation you were facing?

5. **Select a volunteer to read the passage Philippians 4:8–9. Ask the following questions regarding the passage:**

   What are the opposites of each thing Paul says to think about?

   What is the greatest source of those negative things entering your life? (Example: news, social media, unhealthy relationships, etc.)

   How does turning your thought life to what Paul commands bring happiness and peace?

6. **Select a few volunteers to split reading the passage Psalm 19:7–9. Discuss the following questions regarding the passage:**

   What role does reading or studying the Bible play in your life?

   How does mediating on a Bible verse or passage help you fix your thoughts on God?

   Lori teaches that what continually runs through your mind will continually run through your life. How have you found this to be true?

   How does thinking about what you're thinking about help you chase peace?

Close in Prayer

Consider the following prompts as you pray together for:

- Renewed desire to pray and worship in the difficult places

- Minds fixed on that which is right pure, lovely, admirable, excellent, and praiseworthy

- Overwhelming peace

Preparation

To prepare for the next group session:

1. Read Philippians 4:10–23.

2. Tackle the three days of the Session Five Personal Study.

3. Memorize this week's passage using the Beautiful Word Scripture memory coloring page. As a bonus, look up the Scripture memory passage in different translations and take note of the variations.

4. If you've agreed to bring something for the next session's Opening Group Activity, get it ready.

When we rejoice in the *One* who is perfectly happy, we are filled with happiness.

REJOICE IN THE LORD ALWAYS.
I WILL SAY IT AGAIN: REJOICE!

PHILIPPIANS 4:4

SESSION
5

PERSONAL
STUDY TIME

DIGGING INTO THE

BIBLE STUDIES

PHILIPPIANS
CHASING PEACE

DAY 1

PHILIPPIANS 4:4-5

Paul repeats his instruction to "Rejoice!" It's not just a friendly suggestion or something we might want to think about. Rather, "Rejoice in the Lord always" (Philippians 4:4) is an imperative, a directive, a command. Isn't it so kind of God to make rejoicing a responsibility and delight a duty? And Paul doesn't just say, "Rejoice always." He says, "Rejoice in the Lord always." We can rejoice always, no matter what circumstances come our way, when we find our happy in the Lord who is the source of happy.

1. **Read Philippians 4:4. What does it look like for you to rejoice *in* the Lord even in painful circumstances?**

In 1 Timothy 6:15, Paul identifies God as "the blessed and only Ruler, the King of kings and Lord of lords." That word "blessed" in the original language is the Greek word "makarios," which means blessed, happy, or perfectly happy. So Paul is calling God "the perfectly happy and only Ruler."

2. Look up the following passages and complete the chart, noting what each scripture reveals about God being the source of our happiness and blessings.

SCRIPTURE	WHAT THE PASSAGE REVEALS ABOUT GOD AS THE SOURCE OF ALL HAPPINESS AND BLESSING
Psalm 16:8-9	
Proverbs 10:28	
John 15:11	
Romans 15:13	

When there is a command, it also means there's a choice. You can command kids to do their homework. When that directive is issued, it is done for their own good and growth. But it also means they have a choice on whether they're going to follow through in obedience to do their homework.

It's the same for us. God's Word has given us this command to rejoice in Him for our own good and growth. That means we're faced with a choice of whether we're going to follow through in obedience to choose happiness and joy.

3. In the space below, identify an area of struggle. Then, write words of thanks and praise to God for who He is even amid the circumstances.

Struggle:

Words of thanks and praise:

4. Read **Philippians 4:5**. In what current situation are you struggling to be gentle with someone else? Yourself?

Would you rather be treated with strict fairness or abundant kindness? Explain.

5. Read **Matthew 11:28–29**. How has God shown His gentleness to you?

6. In the space below, write a prayer asking God to grow the fruit of gentleness in you.

DAY 2

PHILIPPIANS 4:6-7

We live in a world with billions of reasons to worry and feel anxious. The beloved child who is overwhelmed at school. The bills that are piling up. The conflict at work. The argument with that friend. The health issue you're facing. The scary story you saw on the news. Reasons to worry pelt us every day, and yet, Paul says not to be anxious about anything. Not a single thing. Nothing. Thank goodness he gives us the key to make this possible.

1. Read **Philippians 4:6**. In the space below, make a list of the top five concerns in your life.

- _____

- _____

- _____

- _____

- _____

Place a star by the ones you've been most persistent in taking to God in prayer and underline the ones you've been least persistent in taking to God in prayer.

2. Why are some of your concerns easier to present to God than others?

3. How does Paul's teaching challenge you to bring *all* your concerns, in *every* situation, to God?

If God already knows everything you're thinking and experiencing, why is it still important to take everything to Him in prayer?

> Is anyone among you in trouble? Let them pray. Is anyone happy? Let them sing songs of praise.
>
> **James 5:13**

Some commentators say that the word "prayer" in verse 6 is better translated: a prayer whose essence is worship and devotion. Yes, we need to take our requests to God and ask Him for what we need. But worship plays a key role, because it centers our thoughts and attention on God and His character.

YOU WILL KEEP IN PERFECT PEACE THOSE WHOSE MINDS ARE STEADFAST, BECAUSE THEY TRUST IN YOU.

Isaiah 26:3

4. Reflecting on the list of character traits of God below, take a moment to reflect on how God has revealed Himself to you in this way and give God thanks for each one. Circle the ones that mean the most to you right now.

All-powerful	Compassionate	Ever-present
Faithful	Gentle	Gracious
Good	Holy	Just
Loving	Kind	Merciful
Sovereign	True	Other _____

5. Where are you struggling with ingratitude?

6. Read **Philippians 4:7**. Of all that you're facing in life, what one issue, if resolved, would bring the most peace to your life?

Do you think Jesus can bring you that peace even if the issue is never resolved? Why or why not?

How do you need to experience Jesus as the Prince of Peace?

DAY 3

PHILIPPIANS 4:8-23

With more than seventy thousand daily thoughts, it's easy to get caught up in the negative ones. Yet Paul challenges us to let those thoughts go and instead embrace thoughts that breathe in and exhale the fullness of life in God.

1. Read **Philippians 4:8**. On the continuum below, how hard is it to follow Paul's command?

❶ ····· ❷ ····· ❸ ····· ❹ ····· ❺ ····· ❻ ····· ❼ ····· ❽ ····· ❾ ····· ❿

It's hard for me to stay away from negative, fear-based thoughts.

It's easy for me to focus on all that's good and true.

2. Why do you think gossip, scandals, and scary news attract more attention than noble, good things worthy of reflection?

3. What are three unhealthy things you're focused on right now?

- _____
- _____
- _____

4. **What are three healthy things you can redirect your thought life toward instead?**

- _____
_____

- _____
_____

- _____
_____

5. **What do the following passages reveal about the importance of controlling your thought life?**

Romans 12:2

2 Corinthians 10:5

Proverbs 4:23

How would you be different if you thought about yourself and others the way God thinks?

6. **Read Philippians 4:10–23 to prepare for the next session. Summarize what happens in this passage in two to three sentences.**

Reflection

As you reflect on your personal study of **Philippians 4:4-23**, what are the BEAUTIFUL WORDS the Holy Spirit has been highlighting to you through this time? Write or draw them in the space below:

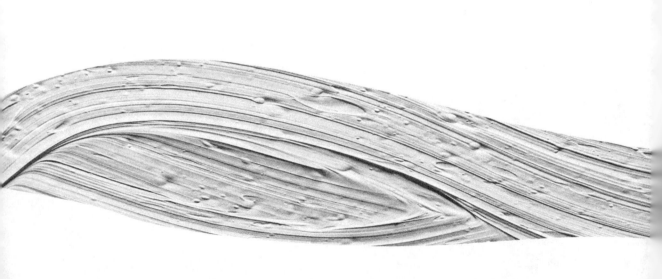

SESSION
6

CHASING
CONTENTMENT

PHILIPPIANS

Opening Group Activity (10-15 MINUTES)

WHAT YOU WILL NEED:

* Each person to bring food to share

* Party balloons or fun decorations

1. Decorate the room with balloons, streamers, wildflowers, and anything else you can find to create a festive atmosphere.

2. Enjoy laughing, talking, sharing, and catching up as you eat together.

3. Discuss the following questions:

What have you enjoyed most about the book of Philippians?

What's one question or topic from the homework or discussion that really challenged you or stuck with you?

Watch Session Six Video (20 MINUTES)

Group leader, stream the video or play the DVD.

As you watch, take notes while thinking through:

What caught your attention? • • • • • • • • • • • • ➤

What surprised you? • • • • • • • • • • • • • • • ➤

What made you reflect? • • • • • • • • • • • • • ➤

Happiness is cultivated in contentment with the provision of God.

The secret to contentment is more appreciation.

The hinge to happiness is Jesus.

Generosity boomerangs joy back into your life.

Giving is about us becoming more like our Savior.

When you begin with grace and end with grace, everything in between is filled with joy.

SCRIPTURE COVERED IN THIS SESSION:
PHILIPPIANS 4:10-23

Group Discussion Questions (30-45 MINUTES)

Group leader, read each numbered prompt and question to the group and select volunteers for Scripture reading.

• • • • •

> "If I'm **honest**, my **want** of more extends way beyond chips and salsa. Maybe yours does, too. We want more **money**. More **house**. More **toys**. More **impact**. More **influence**. More **success**. More. More. More." — Lori

• • • • •

Which of the following would you be most tempted by: more money, more house, more toys, more impact, more influence, more success, or something else? Discuss.

What's one thing where you're tempted to think, *If I only had _____, then I'd be happy*?

How do you balance setting goals and being happy with what you have?

When have you set a goal for accomplishing, achieving, or acquiring more and it became unhealthy?

1. **Select a volunteer to read the passage Philippians 4:10–12. Discuss the following:**

    Where are you in your journey of learning to become content in all things?

    What practical tips have helped you experience breakthrough?

    • • • • •

    "On one hand, you've got: I **can do** all things through Christ. And on the other hand: Apart from me you can do **nothing**. And they both hinge on Jesus. With Him, we can **do all** things, but without Him, we can't do anything. It's Jesus and His **strength** that help us learn how to get along **happily** no matter the circumstance. Because happiness is **cultivated** in **contentment** with the provision of God." — Lori

    • • • • •

2. **How do you find a balance between the truth *you can do all things through Christ* and *apart from Him you can do nothing*?**

    What role does Jesus play in your personal happiness?

    What are practical ways you can cultivate contentment?

Lori teaches that happiness doesn't come from clinging to what you have but from giving what you have. Contentment isn't about getting something new, it's about becoming someone new.

3. **Describe a time when you experienced the boomerang of generosity by receiving joy from giving.**

    How does bringing happiness to others impact your own happiness?

4. **What's an act of generosity that you've sensed the Holy Spirit nudging you to do and resisted?**

    What's stopping you from doing it?

5. **Go around the group and discuss the following questions:**

    How have you been challenged to chase the right kind of happy through your reading of the book of Philippians?

    How would you sum up the message of Philippians and Paul's call for believers to rejoice?

6. **What's your biggest takeaway from this Beautiful Word study?**

    How may the Holy Spirit be empowering you to live differently because of this discovery?

Close in Prayer

Consider the following prompts as you pray together for:

- Greater contentment in Christ

- Opportunities for outrageous generosity

- Wisdom to chase the right kind of happy

Preparation

To conclude:

1. Read Philippians 4:10–23.

2. Tackle the three days of the Session Six Personal Study.

3. Memorize this week's passage using the Beautiful Word Scripture memory coloring page. As a bonus, look up the Scripture memory passage in different translations and take note of the variations.

Happiness is cultivated in contentment with the provision of God.

I REJOICED GREATLY IN THE LORD THAT AT LAST YOU RENEWED YOUR CONCERN FOR ME.

PHILIPPIANS 4:10

PERSONAL

STUDY TIME

DIGGING INTO THE

Beautiful
WORD™
BIBLE STUDIES

PHILIPPIANS

CHASING CONTENTMENT

DAY 1

PHILIPPIANS 4:10-13

Paul concludes his letter to the church of Philippi by thanking them for their gifts and support. Paul, sitting under house arrest in Rome, had a visitor from the church in Philippi. Epaphroditus traveled about eight hundred miles to bring Paul a care package. While we don't know exactly what Paul received, it was probably more than a few muffins or cookies given that it was such a massive road trip. Whatever it was, Paul was grateful for their gifts and encouraged by their concern.

1. Read **Philippians 4:10.** When has someone renewed their interest in you by showing generosity or thoughtfulness?

2. Who is someone to whom you can show generosity or thoughtfulness today?

Renewing their concern for Paul was a big deal. It was an immense effort and great sacrifice. Paul rejoiced in the Lord because he was grateful for their gifts and encouraged by their support, which they'd now had the opportunity to show.

3. Read **Philippians 4:11–13.** The following is a list of signs of discontent. Circle the ones that you wrestle with the most.

Complaining   Nagging   Jealousy

Coveting   Escapism   Grumbling

Disagreeableness   Constant comparing   Other _____

What is necessary for contentment in your life?

4. Look up the following passages. What does each reveal about being content and/or cultivating contentment?

Ecclesiastes 4:8

1 Timothy 6:6–10

Hebrews 13:5

5. Which of the passages is most meaningful to you now? Explain.

The fear of the LORD leads to life; then one rests content, untouched by trouble.

Proverbs 19:23

6. In the following chart, write down any areas of discontentment in your life. Next, write a prayer asking God to meet you in that place. Then, write a word of gratitude to God for who He is and what He's doing in your life.

AREA OF DISCONTENT	PRAYER REQUEST	WORDS OF GRATITUDE

AREA OF DISCONTENT	PRAYER REQUEST	WORDS OF GRATITUDE

A GENEROUS PERSON WILL PROSPER; WHOEVER REFRESHES OTHERS WILL BE REFRESHED.

Proverbs 11:25

PHILIPPIANS 4:14-23

The church at Philippi had been generous with Paul while he was planting the church in Thessalonica. Apparently, people and churches weren't lining up to support the work Paul was doing. But thankfully, giving was an important part of the Philippians' Christian experience right from the very beginning. When Paul was in Thessalonica, the church family in Philippi would have been walking with Jesus for just a few months. Yet, they'd already discovered that generosity boomerangs joy back into your life.

1. Read **Philippians 4:14–16. How would you describe the giving habits of the church in Philippi?**

   How would you describe your giving habits?

2. **What do the following passages reveal about giving and gifts? Circle the one that encourages you the most and underline the one that challenges you the most.**

   Luke 6:38

   Luke 12:33

   Proverbs 11:24–25

   2 Corinthians 9:7

   Hebrews 13:16

The Philippian people weren't wealthy. In fact, giving was a huge sacrifice for them. Yet, Paul says their generosity would be credited to their accounts and reap eternal dividends. When we trust God with what we have and are willing to share what we have for eternal purposes, God will meet our needs and, often, His generosity will overflow and brim over in our lives.

3. Read **Philippians 4:17–20**. When you give, do you tend to view it as a gift to others, a gift to a cause, or a gift to God? Explain.

Do you really think even the smallest gifts can make a difference? Why or why not?

4. What are you doing to store up treasures in heaven?

Where are you struggling to believe God will meet all your needs?

Just as Paul started his letter, "Grace and peace to you from God our Father and the Lord Jesus Christ" (Philippians 1:2), Paul writes his final sentence harkening back to that same grace, saying, "The grace of the Lord Jesus Christ be with your spirit. Amen" (Philippians 4:23). Just like the book of Philippians, when you begin with grace and end with grace, everything in between is filled with joy. Happiness is found inside the grace of Jesus.

5. Read **Philippians 4:21–23**. How does Paul's closing embody what he writes throughout the book?

Where do you most need to experience the grace of Jesus right now?

6. How does chasing contentment empower you to live a better life?

DAY 3

YOUR BEAUTIFUL WORD

Review your notes and responses throughout this study guide. Place a star by those that stand out to you. Then respond to the following questions.

1. **What are three of the most important truths you learned from studying happiness in Philippians?**

   How have those truths set you free?

2. **After reviewing the six Beautiful Word coloring pages, which scripture stands out to you the most? Why?**

3. **What's one practical application from studying happiness and joy in the book of Philippians that you've put into practice?**

> While honest potters discarded flawed pottery, dishonest ones would fill the cracks with wax. To tell the difference, buyers would hold the pottery up to the light, which would expose the trickery. When Paul uses the word "pure" in v. 10, he's referring to that which can be held up to the light and remain whole and true.

4. What's one practical application from the study that you would still like to put into practice?

5. How has the Holy Spirit prompted changes in your attitudes, actions, and behaviors because of studying Philippians?

6. How has the Holy Spirit challenged you to chase the right kind of happy?

Reflection

As you reflect on your personal study of **Philippians 4:10–23**,
what are the BEAUTIFUL WORDS the Holy Spirit
has been highlighting to you through this time?
Write or draw them in the space below:

SMALL GROUP LEADER'S GUIDE

If you are reading this, you have likely agreed to lead a group through *Philippians: Chasing Happy.* Thank you! What you have chosen to do is important, and much good fruit can come from studies like this. The rewards of being a leader are different from those who are participating, and we hope you find your own walk with Jesus deepened by this experience.

Philippians is a six-session study built around video content and small-group interaction. As the group leader, imagine yourself as the host of a dinner party. Your job is to take care of your guests by managing all the behind-the-scenes details so that as your guests arrive, they can focus on each other and on interaction around the topic.

As the group leader, your role is NOT to answer all the questions or reteach the content—the video, book, and study guide will do most of that work. Your job is to guide the experience and cultivate your small group into a kind of welcoming, teaching community. This will make it a place for members to process, question, reflect, and grow—not receive more instruction.

There are several elements in this leader's guide that will help you as you structure your study and reflection time, so follow along and take advantage of each one.

BEFORE YOU BEGIN

MATERIALS

Before your first meeting, make sure the participants each have a copy of this study guide so they can follow along and have their answers written out ahead of time. Alternately, you can hand out the study guides at your first meeting and give the group members some time to look over the material and ask any preliminary questions. During your first meeting, be sure to send a sheet around the room and have the members write down their names, phone numbers, and email addresses so you can keep in touch with them during the week.

FREE VIDEO STREAMING ACCESS

Additionally, spend a few minutes going over how to access the FREE streaming video using the code printed on the inside front cover of each study guide. Helping everyone understand how accessible this material is will go a long way if anyone (including you) must miss a meeting or if any member of your group chooses to lead a study after the conclusion of this one!

A few commonly asked questions and answers:

Do I have to subscribe to StudyGateway? NO. If you sign up for StudyGateway for the first time using **studygateway.com/redeem**, you will not be prompted to subscribe, then or after.

Do I set up another account if I do another study later? NO. The next time you do a HarperChristian Resources study with FREE streaming access, all you need to do is enter the new access code and the videos will be added to your account library.

There is a short video available, walking you through how to access your streaming videos. You can choose to show the video at your first meeting, or simply direct your group to the HarperChristian Resources YouTube channel to watch it at their convenience.

HOW TO ACCESS FREE STREAMING VIDEOS: https://youtu.be/JPhG06ksOn8

GROUP SIZE

Generally, the ideal size for a group is between eight to ten people, which ensures everyone will have enough time to participate in discussions. If you have more people, you might want to break up the main group into smaller subgroups. Encourage those who show up at the first meeting to commit to attending the duration of the study, as this will help the group members get to know each other, create stability for the group, and help you know how to prepare each week.

OPENING GROUP ACTIVITY

Each of the sessions begins with an Opening Group Activity, which you, the leader, should read through and practice prior to your group meeting if it seems new to you.

There are a few questions that follow the activity that serve as an icebreaker to get the group members thinking about the topic for the week. Some people may want to tell a long story in response to one of these questions, but the goal is to keep the answers brief. Ideally, you want everyone in the group to get a chance to answer, so try to keep the responses to a minute or less. If you have talkative group members, say up front that everyone needs to limit his or her answers to one minute.

Give the group members a chance to answer but tell them to feel free to pass if they wish. With the rest of the study, it's generally not a good idea to have everyone answer every question—a free-flowing discussion is more desirable. But with the opening icebreaker questions, you can go around the circle. Encourage shy people to share, but don't force them.

PREPARING YOUR GROUP FOR THE STUDY

Before watching your first video at your first meeting, let the group members know that each session contains three days' worth of Bible study and reflection materials to complete during the week. While the personal study is optional, it will help the members cement the concepts presented during the group study time and encourage them to spend time each day in God's Word. The *Beautiful Word Bible Studies* series is designed so each participant reads through the entire book of the Bible being studied over the course of the personal study exercises. One of the most lamented aspects of all church ministry is struggling to get people to read their Bibles on their own. We have made reading a book of the Bible as simple and engaging as ever and your group members will not believe what they get out of spending time each week engaging God's Word for themselves!

Also, invite your group members to bring any questions and insights they uncovered while reading to your next meeting, especially if they had a breakthrough moment or if they didn't understand something.

WEEKLY PREPARATION

As the leader, there are a few things you should do to prepare for each meeting:

- *Watch the video.* This will help you become familiar with the content Lori is presenting and give you foresight of what may or may not be brought up in the discussion time.

- *Read through the group discussion section.* This will help you become familiar with the questions you will be asking and allow you to better determine how to structure the discussion time for your group.

- *Decide which questions you definitely want to discuss.* Based on the amount and length of group discussion, you may not be able to get through all the questions, so choose four to five questions that you want to cover.

- *Be familiar with the questions you want to discuss.* Every group has times when there are no respondents, and the question falls flat out of the gate. This is normal and okay! Be prepared with *your* answer to the questions so you can always offer to share as an icebreaker and example. What you want to avoid is always answering the questions and therefore speaking for the group. Foremost, encourage members of the group to answer questions.

- *Remind your group there are no wrong answers or dumb questions.* Note that in many cases there will be no one "right" answer to the question. Answers will vary, especially when the group members are being asked to share their personal experiences.

- *Pray for your group.* Pray for your group members throughout the week and ask God to lead them as they study His Word.

- *Bring extra supplies to your meeting.* The members should bring their own pens for writing notes, but it's a good idea to have extras available for those who forget. You may also want to bring paper and additional Bibles.

STRUCTURING THE DISCUSSION TIME

You will need to determine with your group how long you want to meet each week so you can plan your time accordingly. Generally, most groups like to meet for either sixty minutes or ninety minutes, so you could use one of the following schedules:

Section	60 minutes	90 minutes
Introduction (Members arrive and get settled; leader reads or summarizes the introduction.)	5 minutes	10 minutes
Opening Group Activity	5 minutes	10 minutes
Video Notes (Watch the teaching video together and take notes.)	20 minutes	20 minutes
Group Discussion (Discuss the Bible study questions you selected ahead of time.)	25 minutes	40 minutes
Closing Prayer (Pray together as a group and dismiss.)	5 minutes	10 minutes

As the group leader, it is up to you to keep track of the time and keep things moving along according to your schedule. You might want to set a timer for each segment so both you and the group members know when your time is up. (Note: There are some good phone apps for timers that play a gentle chime or other pleasant sound instead of a disruptive noise.)

Don't be concerned if the group members are quiet or slow to share. People are often quiet when they are pulling together their ideas, and this might be a new experience for them. Just ask a question and let it hang in the air until someone shares. You can then say, "Thank you. What about others? What came to you when you watched that portion of the video?"

GROUP DYNAMICS

Leading a group through *Philippians* will prove to be highly rewarding both for you and your group members. However, this doesn't mean you will not encounter any challenges along the way! Discussions can get off track. Group members may not be sensitive to the needs and ideas of others. Some might worry they will be expected to talk about matters that make them feel awkward. Others may express comments that result in disagreements. To help ease this strain on you and the group, consider the following ground rules:

- When someone raises a question or comment that is off the main topic, suggest you deal with it another time, or, if you feel led to go in that direction, let the group know you will be spending some time discussing it.

- If someone asks a question you don't know how to answer, admit it, and move on. At your discretion, feel free to invite group members to comment on questions that call for personal experience.

- If you find one or two people are dominating the discussion time, direct a few questions to others in the group. Outside the main group time, ask the more dominating members to help you draw out the quieter ones. Work to make them a part of the solution instead of the problem.

- When a disagreement occurs, encourage the group members to process the matter in love. Encourage those on opposite sides to restate what they heard the other side say about the matter, and then invite each side to evaluate if that perception is accurate. Lead the group in examining other Scriptures related to the topic and look for common ground.

When any of these issues arise, encourage your group members to follow these words from the Bible: "Love one another" (John 13:34), "If it is possible, as far as it depends on you, live at peace with everyone" (Romans 12:18), and "Be quick to listen, slow to speak and slow to become angry" (James 1:19). This will make your group time more rewarding and beneficial for everyone who attends.

SESSION ONE: CHASING JOY

Scripture covered in this session: **Philippians 1:1–11**

Scripture to study and read this week: **Philippians 1:1–21**

Verse of the Week: In all my prayers for all of you, I always pray with joy (Philippians 1:4).

Discussion Question choices / notes:

Prayer requests

SESSION TWO: CHASING PURPOSE

Scripture covered in this session: **Philippians 1:12–21**

Scripture to study and read this week: **Philippians 1:12–2:1–11**

Verse of the Week: The important thing is that in every way, whether from false motives or true, Christ is preached. And because of this I rejoice. Yes, and I will continue to rejoice (Philippians 1:18).

Discussion Question choices / notes:

Prayer requests

SESSION THREE: CHASING UNITY

Scripture covered in this session: **Philippians 2:1–11**

Scripture to study and read this week: **Philippians 2:1—3:21**

Verse of the Week: Make my joy complete by being like-minded, having the same love, being one in spirit and of one mind (Philippians 2:2).

Discussion Question choices / notes:

Prayer requests

SESSION FOUR: CHASING CHRIST

Scripture covered in this session: **Philippians 3:1–14**

Scripture to study and read this week: **Philippians 3:1–4:9**

Verse of the Week: Further, my brothers and sisters, rejoice in the Lord (Philippians 3:1)!

Discussion Question choices / notes:

Prayer requests

SESSION FIVE: CHASING PEACE

Scripture covered in this session: **Philippians 4:4–9**

Scripture to study and read this week: **Philippians 4:4–23**

Verse of the Week: Rejoice in the Lord always. I will say it again: Rejoice (Philippians 4:4)!

Discussion Question choices / notes:

Prayer requests

SESSION SIX: CHASING CONTENTMENT

Scripture covered in this session: **Philippians 4:10–23**

Scripture to study and read this week: **Philippians 4:10–23**

Verse of the Week: I rejoiced greatly in the Lord that at last you renewed your concern for me (Philippians 4:10).

Discussion Question choices / notes:

Prayer requests

SCRIPTURE MEMORY CARDS

SESSION 1

In all my
prayers for
all of you,
I always
pray with joy.

Philippians 1:4

SESSION 2

The important
thing is that
in every way,
whether from
false motives
or true, Christ
is preached.
And because
of this I rejoice.
Yes, and I will
continue to
rejoice.

Philippians 1:18

SESSION 3

Make my joy
complete by
being like-
minded, having
the same love,
being one in
spirit and of
one mind.

Philippians 2:2

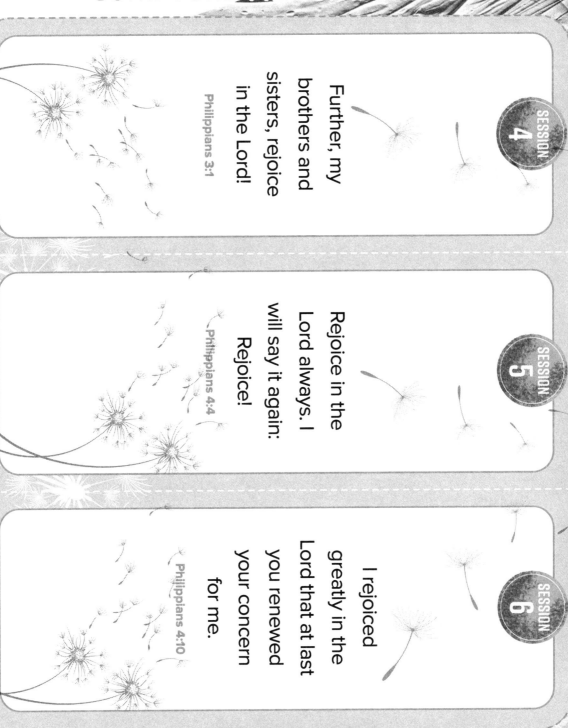

SESSION 4

Further, my brothers and sisters, rejoice in the Lord!

Philippians 3:1

SESSION 5

Rejoice in the Lord always. I will say it again: Rejoice!

Philippians 4:4

SESSION 6

I rejoiced greatly in the Lord that at last you renewed your concern for me.

Philippians 4:10

My favorite thing to do on a lazy afternoon is . . .

When I want a delicious snack, the first thing I reach for is . . .

If there was one place I could travel for a free ten-day vacation, it would be . . .

If I could have a different career, I'd like to be a . . .

My secret dream is to . . .

ABOUT THE AUTHOR

Lori Wilhite serves alongside her husband, Jud, who is the Senior Pastor at Central Church in Las Vegas, which currently has more than twenty-three locations nationally and internationally, including twelve locations inside prisons around the country. She is also the founder of Leading and Loving It, which exists to equip and encourage women in leadership to love life in ministry and impacts more than 20,000 pastors' wives and women in ministry. She is the author of several books and Bible Studies including *Ephesians: Head Held High*. Jud and Lori are the proud parents of two hilarious young adult kids, Emma and Ethan, and one spunky bulldog named Stella. She loves laughing until her sides hurt with friends, reading novels cuddled up under cozy blankets on the couch, and crying during episodes of *Antiques Roadshow*.

leading & loving it

Helping women lead strong and thrive in ministry.

Connect with Founder, Lori Wilhite and the

Leading and Loving It Community through

CONFERENCE
COACHING & COHORTS
TOGETHER COMMUNITY
DEVOTIONS + RESOURCES
FREE TOOLBOXES
and much more.

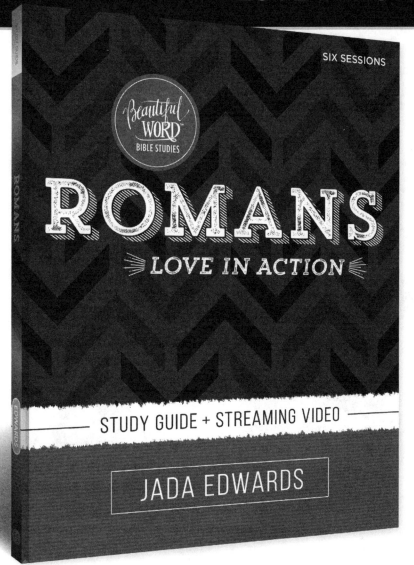

Discover

new
studies

from teachers you
love, and

new
teachers

we know
you'll love!

Explore all these teachers
and more.

SHOP NOW

Kasey Van Norman

Chrystal Evans Hurst

Jada Edwards

Wendy Speake

Christine Caine

Ann Voskamp

Ruth Chou Simons

Bianca Olthoff

Shannon Bream

Dr. Anita Phillips

Lisa Whittle

Karen Ehman

Hosanna Wong

Micah Maddox

Lysa TerKeurst

Rebekah Lyons

Sadie Robertson Huff

Wendy Blight

Madi Prewett Troutt

Jennie Allen

Anne Graham Lotz

Megan Marshman

Lisa Harper

Allison Allen

Margaret Feinberg

Sarah Jakes Roberts

Lynn Cowell

From the Publisher

GREAT STUDIES

ARE EVEN BETTER WHEN THEY'RE SHARED!

Help others find this study:

- Post a review at your favorite online bookseller.

- Post a picture on a social media account and share why you enjoyed it.

- Send a note to a friend who would also love it or, better yet, go through it with them.

Thanks for helping others grow their faith!